The Corporate Detox

The Corporate Detox

Detox

7 FOUNDATIONS FOR CREATING ORGANIZATIONS OF UNPARALLELED EXCELLENCE

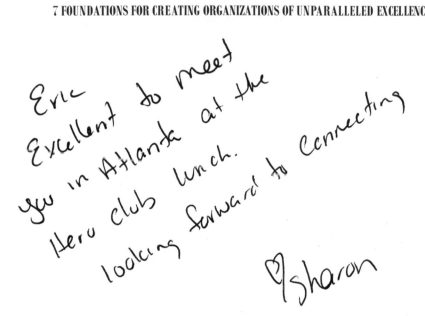

Eric
Excellent to meet
you in Atlanta at the
Hero club lunch.
looking forward to connecting
♡Sharon

SHARON SMITH
C-SUITE RESULTS

CONTENTS

ACKNOWLEDGMENTS

I want to acknowledge all those people who have supported me through my journey. My parents, Carol and Steve Dworkin, have been amazing and never really questioned how I was going to earn a living when I left my successful corporate job—to both of you, I love you and I thank you. To my business support network and accountability partners: you all have a very special place in my heart and life. And to all of you whom I have worked with over the years, both those who showed me what excellence was and those who did not: you may be the most important group because without you I never would have found my calling to serve corporate leaders and to help detox corporate America. Without the leaders who were toxic in my life, I never would have searched for my true calling, so to each of you, thank you for giving me the opportunity to observe and be part of your lives and organizations. I hope that I can serve you in return and help you reach excellence in and beyond the boardroom so that you might see some very sweet results.

INTRODUCTION

T his book is a labor of love to a group I don't think often gets love letters. I'm talking to the C-Suite, the senior executives who get up early, stay up late, make hard decisions every day, and toil over their organizations. You make decisions that affect the bottom line, the shareholder, your employees and their families, your family, your customers, and even your communities. I am writing this for you because you are an underserved population, you have challenges, and you want results. You deserve excellence both in and beyond the boardroom, and I am here to serve you, to tell you that you are not alone, and to show you how things can be easier.

I bet some or all of this rings true for you:

- You are mentally and physically tired from trying to do everything yourself.
- You have struggled with hiring and/or retaining top talent.
- You want your executive team to work with more synergy, energy, and focus.
- You would like to meet your goals faster and with less effort.

- You are ready to be known as an industry leader.
- You want to increase overall productivity and profitability.
- You feel you are leading in isolation and solitude.
- You want to leave a legacy that inspires others to be great leaders.
- You would like to communicate and connect better with your employees.
- You would like to get out of bed with joy and excitement.

The good news is that somehow this book has ended up in your hands. Maybe a friend or coworker gave it to you, or maybe you found it lying around, or maybe you ordered it from my website—that's not what matters. What matters is that you have it. You may be asking, "Why does it matter?" It matters because with the best combination of mind-set, ideas, and tools, you can create much better results than you ever thought possible. After you have spent a little time (it's a little book) reading through it, I think you will agree that you can easily start to implement some small changes and get better results by expending less effort. Whether you want to improve life at home or at work, the steps in this little book are here for you to implement.

To begin to understand where I am going with this, you will want to know about the work I do and the vision I have. My dreams and mission are much bigger than I am, and it will take a radical shift in leadership and a new movement to get the results I am after.

You see, I am on a mission to detox corporate America: that is, to create excellence inside and beyond the boardroom and to watch the next generation of leaders emerge with a new mind-set by which everyone reaps the benefits.

My name is Sharon Smith, and after ten exhausting years as an information-security consultant, traveling around the world and working with hundreds of people across many organizations and industries, I have seen one very common thread. Too many people are working too hard and getting too few results, with far too little joy. This next statement may not be popular with the executive team, but believe me, it is true. You don't have to look far or wide to get the ranks of the employees nodding yes to what I'm about to say.

Corporate America has become toxic. There, I said it. Too many people are just trudging through each day and counting down the hours to quitting time and then counting down the days till Friday. This is not a way to live; this is actually quite depressing to me when I think about it. No kid says, "I want to grow up and be depressed," or "I want to grow up and have the Sunday-night blues." Kids want to grow up and do great things, but then something happens. Many people never experience or realize their potential. Instead, when I ask people how they're doing, I hear, "I'm hanging in there," or "I'm good for a Monday," or "At least it's almost Friday." This is the toxic mind-set that has evolved and spreads through organizations like cancer, killing productivity and engagement.

Another less-than-popular statement is this: I believe that C-Suite and senior executives across all industries (corporate, education, medical, military, and so on) have an obligation to create greatness. At the very top, it is not just about creating profits and increasing shareholder value; it is about your obligation as an elite leader to create organizations of unparalleled excellence and thriving cultures, and to do so with greatness for yourselves and for your employees. Think back to your favorite boss or leader of all time and then compare that person to one you really didn't like—the one who had a tendency to make your blood boil. Who are you more like when your employees think of you? Is it who you want to be—who you intended to be when you started out—or someone very different?

This book is my love letter to you, the C-Suite executive, and to the next generation of leaders who are going to step up and say, "Enough is enough." It's for anyone who wants to be part of a movement that is fed up with leaders who don't care about anything other than how they think they look to everyone else. This book is for the leaders who know that continuing to do what they have always done and expecting different results just doesn't work. And this book is for, as Steve Jobs said it best, "the crazy ones, the misfits, the rebels, the troublemakers, the round pegs in the square holes...the ones who see things differently—they're not fond of rules...You can quote them, disagree with them, glorify or vilify them, but the only thing you can't do is ignore them because they change things...they push the human race forward, and while some may see them as the crazy ones, we see genius, because the ones who are crazy enough to think that they can change the world are the ones who do."

It is time for greatness, it is time to lead with excellence, and it is time for everyone to benefit from great results inside and beyond the boardroom. Are you crazy enough to join me and start a revolution against toxic leadership?

Are you ready to join me in detoxing corporate America and creating a legacy that will have a lasting impact?

If you are ready, let's get started!

CHAPTER 1

THE TRUTH ABOUT YOUR IMPACT

May I be frank with you? There is a problem with employee engagement, and it affects the bottom line. It seems that we keep throwing more technology at business problems when business problems are really people problems. With all the technology we now have, it seems we have forgotten that real people sit behind those computers, behind each e-mail message, behind each decision, and behind all our results. It is time to stop looking for technological answers to business problems, productivity issues, and engagement challenges. It is time to reintroduce the human element of business, and that can only be done by starting with the mind-set at the very top, in the C-Suite.

Since your employees' engagement is one of the key differentiators in your company's success and profits, I think stopping for a minute to discuss this is important. For over fifteen years I experienced and observed what was happening in the trenches, and it wasn't pretty—and that's the truth. I saw employees spending more time talking about what was on TV the night before than doing any real work. I heard people gossiping about the boss or creating rumors because the truth was not told and there was little transparency. I saw necessary changes being overlooked because the boss wasn't willing to admit when he or she was wrong. Much of this was the result of toxic environments. It is time for a change—a big change—and we need a different view on leadership if we are going to detox corporate America.

Let me take a minute and define what I mean by toxic corporate environments. Organizations are not just names on the side of the building or a stock symbol. Organizations are made up of people; they are made up of living organisms, and as such, organizations are also alive. We have seen the birth of new organizations as well as their growth and sometimes their death. How many companies are no longer around that we knew in the recent past? Remember Borders bookstore, Circuit City, Enron, and Arthur Anderson, to name a few? We have seen big names come and go over the years, and now we are seeing mammoth companies that didn't even exist ten years ago. If they don't focus on excellence, however, they most likely won't be around in another ten years; they will be replaced by something new.

Because organizations are made up of people and are indeed alive, it makes sense that, like people, organizations can become toxic. When we talk about people being toxic, most often we are talking about health, disease, and other characteristics associated with the mind and body. When a person says, "I'm doing a detox," most people don't think much about it. We have all heard of a detox. Some associate it with a cleanse based on the food that goes into the body; some think of it as removing drugs and alcohol from the body; for others, a detox can be an emotional and mental cleansing.

A detox for an organization is not all that different except that it addresses more than one person and usually involves a close look at the company culture. The entire organization could need a detox, or it could be limited to a team of leaders, or a team of workers, or a specific department or location. A detox for an organization has to do with cleansing an old mind-set, looking at things very differently, opening up to new ideas, creating a different company culture, thinking about each employee as an asset and a person, and seeing opportunities and solutions rather than problems and blame.

This detox has to start at the top and work its way down. It takes time and work, and it triggers frustration and questions. It takes a strong leader to say, "Yes, let's do this," and stick with it. Like a detox for the body, it doesn't happen overnight. You can't go to the gym for one week, take a pill, and be done. No, you work day in and day out on the changes you want so that you can live a healthier life, and you don't give up on your vision. The same is true here. I am not proposing a magic bullet; rather, I am proposing simple steps you can start to implement today to start achieving better results inside and beyond the boardroom.

—೬

Now, let's get down to brass tacks. I'm not one to sugarcoat the truth. I am going to speak to *you*, the executive in charge of your organization, team, department, or location. We are going to talk like we would if I were sitting in front of you, working with you directly. It does not matter to me whether your organization is made up of ten, one hundred, one thousand, or ten thousand people. Regardless of size, the same root-cause issues exist, and they start with the mind-set of the executive team. Sure, the larger the organization, the more shareholders, and the bigger some of the challenges may be. But at the end of the day, your organization, regardless of size, is made up of people, and those people are the solution to creating the excellence that will help you become an industry leader and define your legacy.

What I want you to understand is that this is much bigger than just your organization. Your decisions and your company culture not only impact your employees but also reach much wider than you could ever imagine. You are probably thinking, "My reach is not that far, my impact is not that big," but let me challenge you on that thought. On average, every employee touches the lives of at least ten people and upward of one hundred people a day. Whether it is on the road, at the supermarket, at their children's school, in the gym, at the doctor's office, or at home—anywhere your employees go, the list of people they impact goes on and on.

Let's look and see how real this is. Think about it: How many people do you interact with every day? I'm talking about those you directly interact with, the lives you touch directly, and those you don't directly talk to, but impact nonetheless. What about the other drivers on the road? Do you think you have an impact on them? Even if you don't directly talk to them or touch them, you impact their lives. Think of the ripple effect of someone having a bad day, and how that person can take it out on all the people around him or her. Your actions toward someone else do not just impact that one person; they impact the people that person comes in contact with too. It is like six degrees of separation (or maybe three degrees in our connected world).

You may not think that the way your employees act outside of work impacts your bottom line, but it does. What happens when employees speak poorly of your organization because they work in a toxic environment? What happens to potential and current customers when they hear from their friends and family (your employees) how much they dislike your company or even you? How many customers might go to your competition because of negativity your employees have about their workplace?

What about unhappy and disengaged employees who are customer facing? Don't they have an impact on the happiness of your customers and your bottom line? For every disengaged employee who does not feel empowered to do more than get to Friday and get paid, there is a customer with whom that employee has dealt and who felt the disengagement of that employee and is now likewise disengaged with your company.

Now, this does not have to be a negative story; this can be turned around because engaged and happy employees also go out into the world, but in a very different way. When you do something kind for someone, it also affects those with whom that someone comes into contact—but in a positive, pay-it-forward kind of way. Actually, the science on this is really amazing: studies have shown that people who just witness a kind act reap the benefit, even when the kind act was not directed toward them.

The impact to your organization by your employees doing acts of kindness creates a loyal following and generates business you may not have imagined before. When your employees speak highly of their workplace, their coworkers, and their bosses, people hear that. When they leave work feeling good, they go out and do good, and people see that. Every action has a reaction, and you can help create positive actions in this world by detoxing your organization and turning it into an organization of unparalleled excellence.

The point I am getting to is both the vision that I have and the greater change that our world needs. We need more people who are paying it forward and creating a positive ripple effect. I don't know whether that is possible, however, given the amount of toxicity there is in corporate America right now. We need a detox that results in creating organizations of unparalleled excellence, organizations that put the human operating system above the technology, organizations where the leaders want more for their employees—in other words, organizations where no one is counting down the day till Friday or just hanging in there anymore.

The next time you are cut off in traffic, stop for a minute and ask yourself: Is this person just an asshole, or is he most likely a good person having a bad day or possibly worried about the day ahead at work? How many times have you driven into work with your mind on something other than the road, and maybe, just maybe, you cut someone off or didn't allow the driver who had had her blinker on for the last quarter mile to merge?

What about at the end of a long, hard day: How do you behave when you leave the office? How do you think unhappy employees behave versus those who leave work feeling empowered about the day they just had and are looking forward to the next one? Remember, this is the result of creating an organization of unparalleled excellence, the result of the vision that I have for a much better version of our corporate culture and country—a vision I would like you to join me in helping to create.

Even if you are an executive leader of an organization that has only ten people, you still impact hundreds, if not thousands, of people. As I mentioned earlier, on average those ten employees will interact with ten other people (or one hundred people), and those people will interact with ten people, and this becomes an exponential number very fast. And if you happen to be part of the C-suite of a much larger organization, think of the extent of your impact on the world. The C-Suite has traditional titles, but leadership crosses all industries regardless of title. You may be a university president, school principal, small business owner, or military leader, but regardless of your title, you are an executive and a leader.

Now, I get that your vision may not be as big as mine, and you may really be most interested in just your organization, and that is completely understandable. This book is still for you because regardless of how big an impact you want to have, you still need to implement new foundations to create change and get the results you want.

―⟲

I would like to share a personal experience with you, one that screams "toxic environment." For several years as a consultant in corporate America, I worked with a "leader" who was that in title only. In my experience, he was abusive and a bully; I was on the receiving end of his emotional outbursts and witnessed others who received the same verbal tirades. As a result, he was unable to retain good talent in his department. When he was not going off on something that he didn't have all the facts on, however, I could see that he was a good person who just didn't know how to say, "I don't know," "I don't remember," "Please help," or "I'm scared." He had not been taught that vulnerability is actually an asset. Instead, he led by command and control, and those around him had very little to no respect for him.

If this man had shown vulnerability and openness it not only would have gained him more respect from his employees and colleagues but also would have given him the freedom to explore what was really needed in any given situation and to learn from everyone around him. Instead, he alienated everyone and got very little done that added value to the organization or the lives of his employees. I would go so far as to say that his inability to admit when things were not going well and to make course corrections cost the company money.

He was not a bad person; apparently, he just never received the tools or education that would have allowed him to understand how destructive his actions were and the impact they had on his team, department, and the overall company culture. No one in that environment felt empowered to tell him what negativity his actions were causing, and I don't think his superiors had the tools to help or provide better examples he could follow. It really was a negative culture created from the top down. This situation, unfortunately, is not unique to this company and is just one example of my observations over the years.

To be fair, I will also share an experience at an organization that really impressed me and was the opposite of toxic. When I spoke with the workers, I could see and feel the cultural difference. I'm talking about the type of job that typically has a very high turnover—the call center employee. I was in this particular call center as a consultant, doing an assessment of their information-security infrastructure and practices. I sat down with a few of the employees to listen to calls they took and to learn more about how they carried out their roles. What I saw and heard really blew me away. The call center empowered its employees to do what they needed to do to make the customer happy. Not the typical, "Sorry, I can't do anything about that" or "Let me check with my supervisor." No, the leadership of this organization had made the environment not only fun to work in but also empowering. I have spoken with and worked with many call center employees over the years, and this was the only time that I could tell they really loved their job and felt they were there to make a difference. And I can tell you that the customers I heard on the calls that day will be back and will not be going to the competition after the service they received.

—⚬

I bet you decided to work hard and make it to the C-Suite because you wanted some power. There is nothing wrong with power; it is neither a bad nor a good thing. But it is something that can be used to get negative or positive results. So let's look at how you can use the power that you have to remove toxicity and create an organization of unparalleled excellence. What will you be remembered for? What long-term value are you adding to the organization, to your employees, to your community, and to the world?

If your goal is to be an industry leader, have a natural competitive advantage, or leave a lasting legacy that would make your kids, parents, and grandparents proud, then you will want to pay attention. Because it is never too late to say, "Wow, what I'm doing may actually be creating toxicity in my organization or, at the very least, is not creating excellence and a legacy of greatness. It's not really working for me the way I want it to, and I'm ready for a change."

In order to lead others in a positive direction, you must first be able to lead yourself. It is OK if you have previously shirked this responsibility or didn't realize that you even had it. I am here to show you the path to results and help you build a new foundation. The results you will achieve are going to create dramatic and sustainable change in your organization, in your life, and in the lives of your employees.

In other words, this is about results in and beyond the boardroom. That means these foundations can help you create excellence both at work and at home—but only if you implement them.

CHAPTER 2

WHY YOUR IMPACT MATTERS

Why does your impact really matter anyway? Why should you start to look at the greater impact that you have? Why should you learn about vulnerability, greatness, and excellence? Why not just keep doing things the way you always have?

Because I know that you want different results, better results, and excellence. I know that you worked hard to get where you are, and you did it for a reason. I also know that when you got to the top, you started to notice that money does not buy happiness; you began to think that maybe there is something else to be done, something that will you bring you joy and excitement while at the same time creating even better profits and results.

Are you familiar with feeling the Sunday-night blues, having a case of the Mondays, celebrating Hump Day, starting the countdown to Friday, and having the TGIF frame of mind? Even if you are not, I guarantee your employees are. This is the status quo for most of them, and it is no way to live life. When this mentality is the norm, you have a workforce of disengaged people just trying to get to the end of the day or week, and it impacts your bottom line. When you disrupt that status quo, however, you get employees who are excited to be at work, focused on getting the work done with excellence and performing fully; you get employees who increase productivity and profitability and impact the big picture.

To illustrate the disengaged workforce I'd like you to take out a one-hundred-dollar bill and burn it. That's right; just light it on fire and watch it burn. You won't do it, will you? So why do it at work? Why let hundreds and thousands of dollars fly out the window due to lack of employee engagement and low productivity?

According to Gallup, organizations with a higher level of engagement report 22 percent higher productivity. In fact, *Forbes* magazine has reported that companies with engaged workers have 6 percent higher net profit margins, and engaged companies have five times higher shareholder returns over five years.

Unfortunately, Gallup has also reported that more than 70 percent of employees feel disengaged in the workplace. We have all seen the signs, such as a lack of enthusiasm—even on your executive team—and a high turnover of your top performers. Are almost three-quarters of your employees just marking the days until Friday rolls around?

What would be possible if your employees were engaged, motivated, and empowered? What would be different? What would change if your employees left work every day feeling a sense of pride and accomplishment, feeling like they are part of something special, something important? How would that impact your business?

I see a world where everyone gets to feel empowered at work. Everyone gets up with purpose each day, and everyone gets to leave work feeling like they accomplished something. I see a world where everyone gets to work toward a greater goal—something bigger than him- or herself—and to be part of something empowering. I have this vision because too many people are just hanging in there and muddling through their day. I have been that person, and I have worked with hundreds of others who are those people—good people who want to contribute more of themselves to what they do and do it in an environment that allows them to thrive at the same time.

This idea of creating excellence applies to everyone; my vision is not exclusive. Whether a janitor, a teacher, a nurse, a police officer, an administrative assistant, a security guard, an air-traffic controller, a human-resource director, a vice president, or a CEO, everyone—and I mean everyone—has the right to be happy, however happiness is defined. When we spend over one-third of our lives working (assuming a forty-hour workweek and a working life of twenty-five to thirty years), that is a lot of time either to create and be part of something extraordinary or to live with the opposite and be miserable.

I'm not saying that all people are in a position to fully pursue their passions and dream careers. After all, we don't all get to become singers, artists, professional athletes, pilots, and so on. But regardless of the work we do, if we are given an environment that honors who we are and empowers us toward a greater good, there is meaning in the work. This becomes one of the foundations you are going to read about in the following chapters.

Maybe creating this kind of culture seems like too much work, too hard, and even a bit scary. How do you become someone who can have a huge positive impact not just on your organization, but on the world? Let's start with asking why you decided to climb the corporate ladder and run the show. Was it just for the money, was it for legacy, was it for ego? Or was it because with great leadership comes great responsibility, and you knew early on that you wanted to do something great? Sometimes we forget why we started on something or lose sight of what we are working toward, and it takes a reminder to get back on track.

If you have fallen off the path and you want to get back on track—or to get started, if you are a new executive—the first thing to do is to declare and set the intention that you want to be the type of leader who leads with greatness and makes a positive impact on the world. That you want to be someone who does big and great things—earning not only better profits and bottom line results for your organization but also big things far beyond the walls of your company.

⎯⦚⎯

I know that as a leader your biggest challenges include vulnerability and transparency. Most leaders I've worked for shy away from wearing their fears, emotions, or lack of knowledge on their sleeve; they shy away from vulnerability. When this happens, a command-and-control environment is created similar to the one I described earlier in this chapter. As humans, we have two choices when we are scared: we can admit it and ask for help (which is the vulnerability that I am talking about), or we can compensate for it and behave as if we know the answer, and anyone who thinks otherwise will be sorry. The second tends to be the most common action I have seen over the years, especially among those in leadership roles. It often sounds like, "It's my way or the highway," "What's broken?" "Who's to blame?" and "Where can I point my finger?"

I believe most of this is learned behavior that stems from our natural survival mechanism. When we were hunters and gatherers, we had to survive against other tribes, wild animals, and the natural elements. We had fight-or-flight impulses all the time, and when we fought it was for survival. As we have evolved, very few actual fight-or-flight scenarios that are life-or-death situations remain, but our brains have not caught up with our modern way of life. I see this reflected in present-day scenarios involving competition. We tend to see people with different views as a threat, and we respond in a defensive way—the fight reaction. Instead of keeping our bodies safe, we are now left with protecting our ego.

Don't worry; it's not all bad. The great news is that with the right tools and knowledge, you can learn to remove the negative components of the ego from leadership so there is no longer a need to fight to protect it. This is a new learned behavior that allows you as a leader to focus on solutions, greatness, and excellence rather than problems, survival, and fighting.

—ᴄᴏ—

You also have an impact on hiring and retaining top talent. How much does hiring and turnover cost? Hiring employees involves paying them a salary, offering them a bonus and benefits, training them, and helping them become a contributing member of the team; it is therefore very costly if they leave. Having that talent leave is expensive because you have to start all over again.

Why do people leave? They leave because they think the grass is greener on the other side. But if the grass is green and lush on your side of the fence, they have no reason to leave, and when they're raving fans, you will spend much less on hiring because your new employees will come from referrals of your current employees. Good employees want more good employees around them and will bring in the best of the best for you.

Talk about a legacy! Picture your office building with a line around it with the best talent wanting to work for you because your current workforce is so happy and engaged that they are not leaving for greener pastures. Why? Because those greener pastures could not possibly exist—yours is the greenest and lushest. What would that do for the bottom line—not to mention what it would do for the world? Happy employees are happy citizens, happy parents, happy spouses, happy friends, and happy neighbors.

I see two options in front of you: One, you can continue reading this book to learn about the seven foundations to achieving excellence in and beyond the boardroom—pick any one of the foundations to start implementing. Or two, you can continue to operate with the mind-set of legacy leadership, the status quo, and hope that your competition doesn't read this book since that may give them the competitive advantage that puts you out of business. I will tell you from personal experience that employees are waiting for a major shift. There are too many disengaged workers who crave more, are hungry to produce more, and have a drive that has gone unanswered. The leaders who take the first step to make the change will be the ones who come out on top. Consumers are tired of bad customer service, they are tired of bad executive behavior, and they are looking for a hero.

Whose hero are you going to be? Will you be a hero to your kids, your family, your employees, your customers, your town, your state, or something bigger? If you could not fail, what would you do differently? Think big and dig deep. What is it that you really want? What legacy do you want to leave behind? Who do you want to be?

CHAPTER 3

RESULTS

I talk a lot about getting different results, detoxing corporate America, and creating organizations of unparalleled excellence. And you can only get different results when you start to take different actions. The actions you take come from your thoughts, your experiences, and your view of the world. If you think you cannot do something, you will not take action toward it. Or you may take action in the opposite direction to unconsciously prove to your ego that you were right not to do it. If you think you can do something, you are much more likely to take action toward achieving it. Also, don't confuse inaction with not taking action because, in this case, thinking about doing something and not doing it (inaction) is still an action that will create your results.

Because I understand the C-Suite leader's desire for results, I created the R.E.S.U.L.T.S. system for my executive clients. It has been designed to help them confidently take the lead in any situation, even when they don't have the answers. Instead of leading through control and command, this system teaches corporate leaders how to get better results, have a more positive impact, have more time, work with less effort, improve profits, and make a bigger difference. Now I want to share the system with you.

Before we look at each of the seven foundations in the system, I want to tell you that a big part of the process is understanding and integrating vulnerability into the boardroom and into your life. This is important—actually, imperative—because all the answers you need are always in the room, and it is perfectly fine if you are not the one who comes up with them. You will gain more respect when you say, "I don't know," and then ask for the input of others. You will also be amazed at how much more is accomplished and how much more fun it is when you allow everyone to participate and use his or her unique gifts, talents, and brilliance, without judgment. Better results with less effort is probably something you want, and we are going to talk about how to achieve that throughout the remaining chapters.

I'm going to share with you pieces of each foundation in the R.E.S.U.L.T.S. system so you can start to create excellence in and beyond the boardroom. I only share a piece of each because I know you are busy. I believe that what you will learn here will give you enough to start implementing change and achieve results and excellence. Also the foundations are not built in a linear order so you do not have to implement them in the order I've laid them out. I do believe, however, that the first foundation should be implemented first, but everything else in the process happens in an order that makes sense for you. Some of it can be accomplished and implemented simultaneously. After all, not much in life happens in a nice systematic, linear fashion—why should this be any different?

Another thought to keep in mind is that you will not get results from things you do not implement completely. It is your responsibility alone to determine whether you are going to implement any or all of these foundations. And as I learned from my business mentor and coach, "imperfect action will always produce better results than perfect inaction."

I've included tools you can use to implement many of the ideas in this book. I've also included exercises you can do on your own if you are not ready to work with someone else yet. These are the same exercises and tools I use with my executive clients. Some are in this book, and others are available in the companion download at http://www.c-suiteresults.com.

—ᴄ

I also want to debunk a few myths about the work I do and some of the topics I address.

Myth 1: "Having a coach is a sign of weakness." I would say, "Tell that to Tiger Woods, Michael Jordan, or Muhammad Ali." Do you think they had coaches? You bet they did; in fact, I bet they have had multiple coaches. That is why they are the best of the best in their respective sports. Why would you, as an executive, be any better than they are and not need the help of a coach? Don't you want to be the best of the best? Actually, let me quote Bill Gates: "Everyone needs a coach. It doesn't matter if you are a basketball player, tennis player, or gymnast. We all need people who give us feedback. That is how we improve." I also like to say that you can't examine your eye without a mirror, and a coach is that mirror for you. As Google CEO Eric Schmidt said about coaching, "One thing people are not good at is seeing themselves as others see them. A coach is really good at doing that for them."

Myth 2: "Men cannot be vulnerable, and women in the C-Suite really can't be vulnerable or they won't be respected." If everyone learns to be vulnerable, it doesn't matter whether you are a man or a woman running the show. When vulnerability comes from a place of respect for everyone else; when it is displayed to show others that you, the leader, are really no different than they are; and when it is exhibited with excellence, I promise it will work for you. I recently read a quote from Walt Bettinger, CEO of Charles Schwab: "With leadership, you make a decision every day about whether you choose to follow someone. And you make it in your heart, not your head. The ability to inspire followership is so different than management, and it requires transparency, authenticity, vulnerability, and all things that are completely unnatural to you when you are trying to build and achieve and accomplish."

Myth 3: "Love should be left out of the workplace and definitely has no place in the C-Suite." But isn't love the best thing in the world? Isn't it with love that so much can be accomplished? Won't your employees do more for you and your organization when coming from a place of love than a place of fear or force? When was the last time you did something great for someone, did something above and beyond, or put all your effort into something when it did not come from a place of love?

Myth 4: "If I want it done right, I need to do it myself." Here is what I say about this myth: How's that working out for you? How many times have you taken on something that consumed all your time and energy because of this idea, when someone else could have done it faster and better? You'll understand what I'm talking about in the next chapter when we look at the first step in the R.E.S.U.L.T.S. system.

—⟨⟩—

Please remember that change does not happen overnight. But I know that if you start implementing even one of the seven foundational steps of the R.E.S.U.L.T.S. system, you will see results. You can pick one and work on it until you have started to master it, and then pick another. All of this takes time, practice, and often failures before you really figure out who you are and start living authentically. When you start to live authentically and lead from a different place, the results will show up. This is as much about self-discovery and self-love that allows you to be the true representation of who you are and to live life full out as it is about business and leadership.

As Dr. Seuss put it so well: "Today you are You, that is truer than true. There is no one alive that is Youer than You."

And lastly, before you dive into the content you are here for, I've ended each chapter with four reflective questions to help you decide whether your next step will be to implement the foundation:

1. What will happen if I do this?
2. What will happen if I don't do this?
3. What won't happen if I do this?
4. What won't happen if I don't do this?

CHAPTER 4

REVEAL

First, I want you to know that you have a unique brilliance and that everyone on your team has a unique brilliance. Everyone, including you, has gifts, talents, and strengths, and no two people have the same exact recipe. Don't you think it would be boring if we were all the same? And if everyone were like me, your accounting books would be a mess, invoices wouldn't get sent out on time, and most travel plans would wait till the last minute; so it's probably a good thing that we all have different talents, strengths, and gifts.

The key, where the magic happens, is in knowing your unique brilliance, your strengths, and your gifts. Then you can look at the members of your team and start to help them know theirs. You have to know what you bring to the table, what you should and should not be doing, before you look at what your team should or should not be doing. We typically spend too much time in life trying to improve areas we are just not good at, working on things that we should not be working on, and expending too much energy with too few results. I spent a long time in this loop, and once I got out of it, everything became more enjoyable and much easier.

The *R* in the R.E.S.U.L.T.S. system stands for "reveal." When you reveal who you are, not only can you start to focus only on areas of your brilliance, you can also start to do work that you really love, which in turn gives you more energy both at work and beyond. How happy would your spouse, kids, or partner be if you came home earlier every day and with more energy? Well, that is possible when you start to reveal your brilliance and start to work only in that area. Everything else can be delegated to those on your team who have the best capacity—that is, the most energy for each task that you should not be doing.

Because we are all unique, we are not all meant to do the same type of work, to learn the same way, to think the same way, to communicate the same way, or even to show and receive love in the same way. Unfortunately, most schools don't teach us any of this, and depending on what our parents and friends know, we may or may not learn how to be authentic at a young age. We often are fighting an uphill battle or taking the path of greatest resistance because we are trying to do what everyone else is doing, what our parents, teachers, and friends told us to do. Instead of focusing on our strengths, from a young age we are forced to try and improve those areas we are weakest in with the least amount of return for the effort put in. It's time to forget what you learned and become more aware and more authentic, to reveal who you are and how you are wired so that you can start taking the path of least resistance.

My two favorite tools for revealing your brilliance and gifts are the Core Values Index (CVI) assessment (a product of Taylor Protocols Inc., Tukwila, Washington) and the Gallup StrengthsFinder assessment. You can take the CVI on my website at www.c-suiteresults.com/resources/ for free, and you can go to www.gallupstrengthscenter.com to take the StrengthsFinder for fifteen dollars (at the time of this writing). Start with just the top five strengths because that will be enough for you to focus on at first and will be very revealing. When I first saw the results of both the CVI and the Gallup StrengthsFinder, all of a sudden the last twenty years made sense, and I found new ways to use my talents, skills, and brilliance in the work I do now.

The CVI is designed both to show you how you are wired and the energy you have the most and least capacity for and to help you understand your conflict strategies and triggers. For example, I am wired for visioning much more than I am for black-and-white thinking or doing systematic work. This explains why I never enjoyed my work as an auditor or information-security consultant and why I love coaching. With coaching I get to create a vision for myself and for my clients, and I don't have to do the same thing day in and day out in a systematic way like I used to. The Gallup StrengthsFinder will help you understand your top five strengths or, as I prefer to think of them, gifts. With that understanding, you can start to spend more of your time and energy improving your gifts and less time forcing energy on areas that are not your strengths. For example, according to the Gallup StrengthsFinder, most of my strengths are in "Relationship" and "Influencing," with a tiny bit in "Strategic Thinking." Those are areas I can excel at. In my top five I have no strengths in the area of "Executing," however. I'm not going to fight that. Instead, I'll hire and partner with people who are strong in execution and strategic thinking.

Of course, lots of other tools and assessments are out there, but I can't speak to them because they are not the ones I currently use. I have taken the Myers-Briggs Type Indicator, the DISC Personality Assessment, and the Kolbe A & B indexes, and they all provide different values. I'm here to help you focus on your brilliance, and I personally like and use the CVI and Gallup StrengthsFinder when working with clients. I do know individuals who can help with the other assessments, so you can reach out to me for referrals on these other assessments as well as the assessments I offer. I'm here to help you whether you work with me or not.

If you don't want to spend money on a tool, you can start to do this on your own. Take out a piece of paper and draw the following unique brilliance chart. I first learned about this from Fabienne Fredrickson of the Client Attraction Business School, my business coach and mentor at the time.

Unique Brilliance	Excellence
Competence	Incompetence

Unique Brilliance includes the activities you are recognized for being brilliant at. These are the activities you would do for free all day long and still feel like you're having fun. This is what you have a passion for and something you keep getting better and better at.

Excellence is what you're recognized for being excellent at, but you don't have a lot of passion for. After doing these activities all day, you are honestly pretty drained.

Competence is not your strong suit; you are OK at these activities, and you can do them, but they are not your favorite things and someone else could probably do them better than you can.

Incompetence are the things you really stink at, and if you were to never have to do them again, you would be a very happy person and your business would be better off.

Time to brainstorm and fill out each quadrant. Make a list for each category and don't stop until you have filled them all in. Even the smallest things you do—both inside and outside the office—belong in this matrix. If doing dishes or vacuuming belongs in one of these quadrants, put it there. You can even ask those around you to help. Ask your assistant to name the top three things you should not touch. Have fun with it so he or she does not feel awkward answering the question. Ask for the top three things you are brilliant at as well. (You may want to start with the positive, as it will be more comfortable for your assistant to tell you what he or she thinks you are good at than to tell you what you are not so good or stink at.)

Once you have the entire matrix filled out, here is what I want you to do.

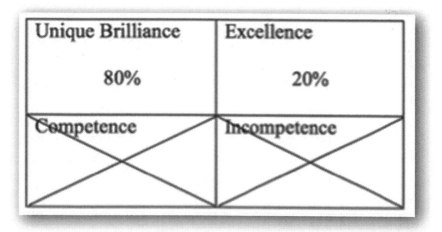

Start by dedicating 80 percent of your time and energy to the strengths you listed under "Unique Brilliance," 20 percent to those listed under "Excellence," and 0 percent each to those in the "Competence" and "Incompetence" categories. Delegate, outsource, hire someone else, or do whatever it takes to stay out of those bottom quadrants. Just make sure that the people you delegate have those tasks in their top two quadrants, or you will just be passing on the misery. Now, this does not mean you get to go home and tell your spouse, partner, or roommate that you are never doing the dishes again. It means you get to have a good open dialogue about what you should be doing at home, what others should be doing, and what you should be bringing in someone else to do.

The reason why understanding who you are and how you are wired is so important is that you can nurture and improve your strengths and get better results instead of trying to improve your weaknesses. It does not matter how hard I work at math or science, I will only get a small return on my investment of time because those topics are not part of my unique brilliance or my excellence. I can work really hard to try to organize and systemize my life, but I'll get frustrated and only get diminishing results for the amount of time I spend because that is not how I'm wired. I can, however, spend time improving my writing, speaking, and communicating, and I will see huge improvements because those are my strengths and my gifts. Stop spending time, money, and energy on things you are not that good at and start investing those same resources in improving your skills, talents, gifts, and brilliance. Do the same for your executive team, employees, and partners. The results will be noticeable and fast.

In order to use your time and energy in a way that creates excellence for you and those around you, it is imperative that you know who you are as well as what your strengths and gifts are. Remember that everyone possesses a unique combination, or recipe, and no one can be just like anyone else. When you try to be like others or think you are supposed to be a certain way, you stop being authentic and really lose the real you in the process.

Remember, this applies to those around you as well. Don't expect them be just like you. Start to learn who they are, what drives them, and what you can do to support their brilliance.

As I previously mentioned, here are four questions that you can ask yourself to help determine if this foundation is something you want to implement.

Ask yourself:

1. What will happen if I do this?
2. What will happen if I don't do this?
3. What won't happen if I do this?
4. What won't happen if I don't do this?

CHAPTER 5

EXCELLENCE

"Excellence," what the *E* in R.E.S.U.L.T.S. stands for, is the next foundation. How you do anything is how you do everything. The question is this: Are you doing everything—or anything—with excellence?

When I say excellence, I mean that everything you do should be done with integrity, with intention, and with quality. You want to be in the top 5 percent, not the mediocre 95 percent. When I say excellence, I also mean brilliance, which we have already discussed, as well as that which will make you and your organization stand out from the crowd. Who do you want to be? Where are you going? What is your vision of the future? Who do you want to be in that future vision? Your mind-set is a big piece of your excellence, and what you think about and what you focus on are what you will continue to bring into your life. Are you focusing on excellence or something less than that?

When you have a clear picture of where you are going, what you want to achieve, and who you need to be in order to achieve it, you can start to make plans, create strategies and tactics, and get your team on board with your vision. Your vision must become their vision, so it must be greater than just you. No one is going to jump on board and give it his or her all if your vision is to make a million dollars and buy a ski lodge in Vail, Colorado. That is a great outcome for you, personally, and something you can achieve, but if you want the power of your team, organization, and community behind you, the vision they will get on board with has to be excellent and much bigger than you—and even bigger than them.

Having a vision that is bigger than you is scary, but it is also more possible because more people will be there to make it happen. Greatness happens when you step outside your comfort zone, so choose a vision that will stretch you and create growth for you.

Another reason to have a crystal-clear vision is that work is hard, and when you don't have a clear "why" behind what you are doing—a clear purpose, a clear mission, and a clear vision—it is very easy to give up. I have done that for sure, and I bet you have too. Sometimes we get excited about something new, but if we don't get crystal clear on why we are doing it or the excellence we plan to achieve from this goal, it is very easy to be done with it when it gets tough.

Have you ever heard of *The Strangest Secret?* It is a book written by Earl Nightingale in 1956, and let me tell you, it's what a lot of other greats have based their work on. Ever hear of *Think and Grow Rich?* Of course you have. Well, what Napoleon Hill and Earl Nightingale both are talking about is the law of attraction. The seed that you plant in your mind, the seed that you water, is the plant that will grow. Your mind does not care whether you plant the seed of something beautiful or something poisonous; nature will produce whatever you plant and whatever you feed in the fertile ground that is your mind. Therefore, excellence begins with your thoughts, your visions, and your desires. Be careful what you wish for, because it just may come true.

I want to talk a bit more about mind-set and how it creates excellence. A good place to start with this concept is by looking at scarcity versus abundance. It's the old idea of whether the glass is half full or half empty. Seeing the glass as half full focuses on abundance—what you do have and what you are grateful for. Seeing the glass as half empty focuses on scarcity—what you don't have. What you think about is what you will bring into your life. Do you want abundance or scarcity? I know that for many people this small shift is not so small. If you have spent years or even your entire lifetime focused on scarcity—what you don't have or what everyone else has that you want (or lack)—this is not a small task. Start small by just observing your thoughts around abundance versus scarcity and remember that anytime you are focused on what you don't have, you are focused on scarcity. You can quickly flip it around to abundance, however, by being grateful at this moment for what you do have.

~6

Excellence also includes who you surround yourself with. Are you surrounding yourself with other people who want the same sort of excellence you want? Birds of a feather flock together, so take good stock in who you surround yourself with—at work, at home, and in social settings. If the people you are spending your time with are negative and don't have the same excellent ambition you do, they are going to drag you down. You are going to remind them of everything they are not, and that is no good for them. The natural thing humans do is protect their ego, so these people who don't consciously mean you harm are going to do everything they can to keep you at their level so that they are not constantly reminded of all they could be doing but have chosen not to do.

If you have a toxic executive on your team, you can get coaching for him or her and a chance to turn it around, or you can ask that person to leave. You cannot keep that executive as one of your key people, though, if he or she is not in the same state of mind when it comes to excellence, your mission, and your vision. The same is true for your friends and those you spend your time with. If they are not lifting you up and going places you want to go, they are probably holding you back from true excellence in life.

—⟆

So the questions I'll put to you now are these: Do you know where you are going, who you need to be to get there, and who you need to surround yourself with? Do you have a clear vision of your future success? Once you do, you can start to set priorities and make decisions based on what will help you get there. When you know where you are going, you have a much deeper understanding of your "why." My favorite tool that I like to use with my clients around this topic is a personal mission statement. Because it is a multistep tool it is not well suited for presentation here, but you can get started with it in the companion download for this book available at www.c-suiteresults.com. Once you complete the first step you can schedule fifteen minutes with me to complete the mission statement by sending an e-mail to me, with the words "Mission Statement" in the subject line, at sharon@c-suiteresults.com.

An exercise you can start right now to do on your own is journaling. I know that most people reading this book are not currently into journaling, but I'll tell you what, it's worth having a go at because it can make a huge difference in your life and your business. The exercise here is about creating a clear vision for where you want to be in three years. Did you know that you will overestimate what you can accomplish in one year, but you will underestimate what you can accomplish in three?

⸺ formula ⸺

Journaling Exercise: Using paper and pen or your computer, spend as much time as you need to just write, without editing or overthinking it. I recommend setting a timer so you have a specific end in front of you. You can start with five minutes if this is new for you, or you can write until you have accomplished a certain number of words or pages. Maybe 250 words, or one written page, is a good start if you have never done this before.

Before you start writing, close your eyes and take a few deep breaths in through your nose and out through your mouth. OK, go ahead. I'm not going anywhere…Great, now that you are a bit more relaxed, these are the ideas to write about in your future vision. Create your ideal perfect day in the future. Not a special day, but what your average day would look like in the future of your design. Consider the following questions:

- You wake up. Where are you? What do you see? Who do you see? What do you smell?
- You get out of bed. Where do you go? What do you do? Who do you talk to? What do you talk about?
- How does your day progress from there? What do you do for work? Who do you work with? What is around you? What can you touch, taste, and smell?

- What is for lunch? Where do you have lunch? Who are you with? What are you talking about?
- What do you do in the afternoon (be specific)?
- What about dinner? What do you taste and smell? Who are you around? Where are you? What do you hear?
- What is the evening like? What happens before bed? What are you excited about for the next day?

Picture it all from beginning to end; all the colors, the smells, the sounds, the people, the conversations, the work, the fun, the joy. Imagine everything that makes this the perfect average day in the life of your creation, everything that makes it excellent. You can do this exercise regarding your business also. You can write specifically about what you see when you walk into the office, who greets you, what you smell, what you say, what you do first, and so on. Now that you have a clear vision of what you want and where you want to be, you can start creating strategies to get there.

Time to check in with yourself.

As it relates to this foundation:

1. What will happen if I do this?
2. What will happen if I don't do this?
3. What won't happen if I do this?
4. What won't happen if I don't do this?

CHAPTER 6

SELF-AWARENESS

The first *S* in R.E.S.U.L.T.S. stands for "self-awareness," and it is going to become your best friend in business and in life. When you become more self-aware, the results you will achieve are going to amaze you. Self-awareness has to do with observing and understanding your internal energy and your energy blocks. Once you start to observe and understand what is blocking you, you can learn how to remove those blocks and get better results.

When I refer to energy blocks, I am talking about thought patterns that drain your energy and take you into a mind-set that can sabotage all your good work. Most of this occurs at a subconscious level, and that is why you must become self-aware to understand what is going on. It is happening whether you know it or not, but you can only do something about it when you start to pay attention and observe these thoughts and energy blocks. If you do not begin to think differently, you will not act differently and you will not get different results.

One of the biggest energy blocks I find is simply whether we are focused on the future, the present, or the past. The thing to understand is that "now" is all you have. You cannot live in the past or the future. The challenge is that most people do not learn to be mindful and present in the place and moment where they are. Living in the now is where you'll find peace, creativity, and the greatness you are capable of.

You can learn from the past and plan for the future, but you can take action only on what is happening today, right now. Too much time spent in the past can lead to depression, and obsessing about what might happen in the future can keep you in a constant state of anxiety. You cannot come up with new brilliant and creative ideas if your mind is not connected to the present moment.

Does this sound a bit trivial? Let's look at it in terms of dollars and cents. Estimate how many hours you spent yesterday, or last week, or last month, thinking about the past or worrying about the future. Or start to track it going forward to get a more accurate figure. Then, determine what you are worth per hour (the amount you make or want to make divided by 2,080-the number of hours a person works based on 40 hours a week for a year). Multiply your hourly rate or hourly worth by the number of hours you spent thinking about the past or the future. How much did you spend? What did those thoughts cost you? Chances are, none of those thoughts made you money or otherwise served to move your business forward.

Your thoughts lead to your actions. The effect of your awareness correlates to your effectiveness as a communicator, connector, and leader. The good news is that when you start to observe your thoughts, you can change them. Instead of spending hours thinking about nothing that serves you and wasting lots of money, start to focus your attention on your thoughts. Become more aware and observant of what you are thinking about. When you notice you are dwelling on the past, stop yourself and bring yourself back to the moment. It is great to learn from the past, but spending a lot of time there or dwelling on or wishing for a different outcome does not serve you. It does not make you money, it does not move you forward, and it does not create excellence.

Anticipating and thinking of the future is something I'm probably guiltier of than dwelling on the past. I'm not talking about having a clear vision of what you want your life to look like, as we talked about in the previous chapter. I am talking about playing out scenarios in your mind about how a situation, conversation, or event will go. I'm talking about those conversations we make up between us and others that most likely—actually, I'm going to say with near 100 percent certainty—will never play out the way you create them in your mind. When you start to pay attention to these conversations and thoughts, you must *stop* and bring yourself back to the present. Of course, you can and should plan for events and conversations. You may even have to determine what you want to say in different situations, but spending time other than for basic planning is definitely not time well spent.

You can use journaling here too. You can create a journal where you simply note each time you catch yourself anywhere other than the present. You can write down how your thoughts were blocking you from being in the present and how moving to the present helped you get to a place of creativity and innovation. This exercise of writing down the moments you notice your mind shifting will help you become more aware, shift faster in the future, and stay more present at all times.

I would also like to talk about four specific energy blocks at a high level. They are limiting beliefs, interpretations, assumptions, and gremlins. It was a big eye-opener when I learned about these during my coach training at the Institute for Professional Excellence in Coaching. These are all at the core of your thoughts, and your thoughts create your actions or inactions. Being aware of these four energy blocks and starting to take action to remove them will bring you even greater results at work, at home, and in life.

A **limiting belief** is the thought that you cannot do something that other people can do. It is a thought that limits you. If I said I could not write a book, even though lots of other people have, that would be a limiting belief on my part. If you say you cannot speak at a conference, but other people have and do every day, that is a limiting belief. There are hundreds, if not thousands, of examples of limiting beliefs. They can be about work, leadership, home life, relationships, parenting, travel, hobbies, sports, or anything and everything. Anytime you say, "I can't do that," and someone else has done it, you are expressing a limiting belief.

Now, if you don't want to do something and you say, "I won't do it," that is different. It is still a decision that will block you from moving forward, but at least it is a conscious choice. "I won't write a book" is very different from "I can't write a book." Saying you won't speak at a conference, won't ask someone out on a date, won't travel to Africa, won't run a marathon, and so on are all very different from saying you can't do any of those things.

So the next time you say, "I can't," first stop and ask: "Who says? Why does that have to be true? Where does that belief come from?" After some deeper analysis, you will either determine that it is a limiting belief and that you can or you will make a conscious, well-informed decision not to do something, even if it could make a difference in your career, business, or life. I have a lot of respect for conscious decisions, so start by removing limiting beliefs and being more self-aware of why you are not doing certain activities.

Next come **interpretations**. An interpretation is an energy block that happens when we make up a story about a situation. For example, you may say that you weren't hired because you're a woman or that your book wasn't read because someone thinks you're stupid. An interpretation is your story about a situation when there could be five or ten other answers. Maybe you weren't hired because you weren't the most qualified, or maybe the employer was looking for someone who had done the exact job before. Maybe someone didn't read your book because that person just had other things to do.

I remember sending an e-mail to a company on a topic that I felt was very important. Of course, when I did not get a response as quickly as I wanted, I thought it was because they didn't think it was important and they just didn't care. A good friend and coach of mine at the time said: "What's another reason they haven't responded? What's another story that makes as much sense here?" It took her helping me with the answer to realize that maybe the person I sent it to just had not read it yet. Maybe he was out of the office; maybe he was working on other stuff; maybe he was looking into it. Any of those scenarios were as possible as the story I had made up, but my story was an energy block because it closed me up and stopped me from moving forward. So when you make up a story, ask yourself what someone else might say about the exact same situation. What might be another story that could be as true as the one you're making up right now? Which story do you want to believe? Which one will serve you and help you move forward in a positive direction?

The third energy block—and one that becomes more powerful than the first two are—**assumptions**. These are the thoughts or beliefs that because things happened a certain way before, they will happen that way again. Assumptions let the past dictate your future. When you say something won't work because you've tried it before, you are making an assumption. Saying "Last time I asked Sally on a date she said no, so that means she will say no again" is a simple example of an assumption.

Of course, you want to use past experiences and lessons learned to help guide your future decisions, but you need to look at why you are saying no to something if you are basing that decision on the past. Ask yourself why it has to be the same this time. What was it about the last time that didn't work and you could do differently this time?

The last and most powerful of the energy blocks are the **gremlins**. A gremlin is that ugly voice in your head or the devil on your shoulder telling you that you are not good enough, not deserving enough, not smart enough, not pretty or handsome enough, and so on. This voice has been there for a long time, stopping you from doing big things. This is the hardest of the energy blocks to remove, but you can start by listening for the voice, and the theme, and then saying, "Screw you." You can even name your gremlin so you can call it by name when you tell it to go take a hike!

The point to all of this is to start making more conscious decisions, to take actions based on thoughts that serve you rather than thoughts that are negative energy. Every thought has an energetic consequence. When you start becoming more self-aware of your thoughts, you can start to take actions that will not only serve you better but also serve your organization, your employees, your family, your friends, and your community.

⟿

Another practice that is key to self-awareness is meditation or centering. It is becoming more mainstream in corporate America, but if you have not yet embraced it, take a quick look at why you may want to reconsider. Meditation is a way to connect body and mind, which over time will help you listen to and understand what your body is telling you. Self-awareness is about changing your conscious thoughts as well as understanding what your physical body may be telling you about your subconscious thoughts.

Those feelings of anxiety, those butterflies, or the lump in your throat are all physical signs your body uses to tell you that something in your thoughts—maybe even in your subconscious—is off. Sometimes we notice the physical signs, especially when they are big ones, but often there are smaller signs that we miss. Even joint pain, back pain, digestive issues, sleep issues, and headaches are physical signs that something in your subconscious is not healthy.

When you take time to meditate, you learn to quiet your mind and hear your body and soul. Meditation does not mean you have to sit cross-legged on the floor and make lots of strange sounds. It does not take long periods of time, and you don't have to travel to the Far East or join a temple. Meditation has been associated with many religions, but that does not mean it has to be spiritual for you unless you want it to be. In the most general definition, meditation is a way of taking control of the mind so that it becomes peaceful and focused and the meditator becomes more aware.

In her article titled "How Meditation Benefits CEOs" (*Harvard Business Review,* December 14, 2015), Emma Seppala included building resilience, boosting emotional intelligence, enhancing creativity, improving relationships, and sharpening focus among the benefits of meditation for businesspeople and CEOs. (Interested readers can access the article at https://hbr.org/2015/12/how-meditation-benefits-ceos.)

Meditation is finding a practice that works for you. It is finding a place and time that you can be still and quiet your mind from all that chatter, all those energy blocks, and all the negativity that seems to find its way in. There are a ton of resources on the Internet that you can use to find a meditative practice that works for you. I honestly think that starting with five to ten minutes a day is best. Maybe start with three days a week and work up to five and then seven days. You can use some relaxing music, use guided meditation, or be in complete silence. I have provided some guidance and resources in the companion download to this book found at www.c-suiteresults.com. Remember, it is a practice because it is not easy. You are not used to quieting your mind. Don't beat yourself up if thoughts keep coming to you during your meditation. Acknowledge them and let them go. Keep at it, and over time you will find more and more quiet space between the thoughts.

Not only is meditation good for the mind and self-awareness, but studies conducted by the federal government, Harvard University, the Mayo Clinic, and many more sources have found benefits from and medical uses for meditation. People use meditation for various health problems, such as anxiety, pain, depression, stress, insomnia, and physical symptoms associated with such chronic illnesses as cancer, heart disease, and high blood pressure. Additional benefits to practicing meditation on a regular basis include an enhanced ability to effectively produce visualization and mental imagery, better oxygen circulation, improved digestion, increased energy, general relaxation, improved sleep, decreased physical and emotional pain, reduced fear and anger, a reduced effort of the heart, lengthening of life, and a pathway to feeling a personal spiritual connection.

What do you have to lose? If it is good enough for Hugh Jackman, Clint Eastwood, Howard Stern, Ellen DeGeneres, Steve Jobs, George Lucas, Lenny Kravitz, Dr. Oz, and Google, I bet it is good enough for you.

Time to check in with yourself.

As it relates to this foundation:

1. What will happen if I do this?
2. What will happen if I don't do this?
3. What won't happen if I do this?
4. What won't happen if I don't do this?

CHAPTER 7

UNDERSTAND

The next foundation I will share with you is to *understand* what is distracting you. (The *U* in R.E.S.U.L.T.S. stands for "understand.") I know many people say, "If I just had more time I could get it all done." Or they say, "I'm just no good at time management; there is always too much to do, but not enough time." What if I could tell you that you never have to think about time management again? What if I told you that it does not exist and that you have been working too hard for too long? What if you could understand how to remove distractions and get more done in less time?

We all have the same twenty-four hours in the day, but some people are very successful with that time, and others feel like they spent the day busy as hell with no results to show for it (the busy-being-busy syndrome). The difference between these two groups is that one (those who are successful with their time) understands how to manage priorities, while those who are busy being busy have not clearly defined their priorities. This results in saying yes to everything, taking on tasks that have nothing to do with their end goals or vision, and working entirely too hard with far too little to show for it. The choices you make about how you spend your time directly correlate to your overall success in business and life.

So how do you go from busy being busy to being fully productive with your day? That is, someone who, at the end of the day, has accomplished a lot, still has energy, and is ready to leave the office with excitement for home life? You start by understanding and determining what your priorities are. Remember, the definition of a priority is something that is more important than something else. If everything has the same level of importance, you have no priorities. If reading e-mail has the same level of importance as working on money-generating activities, you may be focused on the wrong activities and may not have any priorities, or the priorities you have may not be ones that will create the results you want.

Once you have defined your top three priorities, you will start to say yes only to tasks that align with one of those three priorities. You will say no to, or delegate, everything else; getting anything else done should not be your main concern. If it is a priority for your business—accounting, for example—finding someone else who can do it will be a much better use of your time, money, and energy. This also goes hand in hand with your brilliance. Your priorities should be what you are uniquely brilliant in doing.

The point is that when you focus only on your top three priorities, everything becomes easier because you easily know what to start saying no to. Once you do this and get used to it, you will really start to like how it feels. It does not mean things do not get done; it means someone else does those things and they become that person's priority. As the leader of your organization, department, team, family, or other group (big or small), you determine your top three priorities. You have everyone else do the same. We can call these your big rocks—those items that you are focused on; that get your attention; and that you base your goals, strategies, and tactics upon. When you do this, you stop tolerating and start living.

In chapter 9 we look at how to break down your goals into smaller, more manageable strategies and tactics. From there you can more easily determine your priorities for each day, week, and month. You may have three big priorities for the quarter that break down into a whole bunch of tasks. Some of those tasks may be within your area of brilliance, and many of them will not be. You will delegate the ones that are not to others and ensure that they also understand the concept of priorities and saying no to other requests.

Then you have what is left: namely, the tasks that you and only you can do. The tasks that are money-generating activities that, when completed, will lead to excellence. Then each of those tasks gets prioritized, and each day, week, and month, you determine what three priorities you are going to work on, and that is what you do. You work on those and say no to everything else. How does that sound?

Are you visual? Do you like having something to prompt you to do this every day? Maybe something you can also use for your team? You can go to the companion download for this book at www.c-suiteresults. com and grab a copy of a daily/weekly/monthly priority e-mail that you can send to your team (including you) to fill out each morning so everyone knows what to focus on and can easily say no to anything else. Remember, this becomes a cultural change. You teach your team that saying no is acceptable if the task is not on their priority list, and if it is something that needs to get done, they can add it to the list for the next day. This means everyone understands that hearing no from someone else is acceptable. You can create boundaries and rules for the few exceptions to this policy.

⌒

I know there are lots of distractions that happen and it's easy to say squirrel or start chasing the next shiny object, trust me when I say I understand. Here are a few ideas to help you tackle some of those common distractions you encounter. If e-mail is distracting, you can set up blocks of time during which you will check e-mail; ensure that everyone understands that you will respond during those times and that emergencies must be handled by picking up the phone. You can add that information to your signature line. It is a great way to set expectations and boundaries. You can have your entire team do the same. Here's another great tip I read once, but I don't remember where. This little tip is something that would have to be taught and become part of your culture : Add NNTR to the end of an e-mail or in the subject line to indicate to the recipients that there is "No Need To Reply." It seems that in our technology- and e-mail-centric world we feel a need to reply with at least a thank-you or some sort of affirmative. But those extra e-mails don't actually add value, and they take time to write and read.

What about your values? Do you know and understand what they are? Your values help you say yes and no to things in a manner that serves you and keeps you energized. When you are doing tasks or working toward something that is not in line with your top values, I bet it drains your energy and makes you feel less than optimal. Not being aware of your values is also a reason why goals often go unfinished and you end up doing things you tolerate rather than things you really enjoy.

Your values serve as a navigational beacon to keep you on course. Just like a ship, if you and your company don't have directions, a good crew, a map charted out, and the equipment you need, the chances of getting to your final destination are slim and the chances of getting ship-wrecked are high. In this analogy, your values and your priorities are each part of the navigation system. One may be the GPS and one may be the map in this analogy, but both values and priorities must be clearly de-fined. You see, I often find that people are doing more work in areas that are not of high value to them and less work in areas that are important to them. Both of these situations cause people to have less energy than they deserve and more stress. Not only do they suffer, but I bet those around them do too. If you had more energy, would your family notice and enjoy time with you more?

Here's an exercise I love doing with my clients: First, read over a list of values and rate them from most to least important. (You can visit the companion download for this book at www.c-suiteresults.com to obtain a list that I use.) Then go back through the list and rate how much action you take based on or in support of each value. If you're like most people, you'll find high action ratings on values that are not that meaningful to you. That means you are tolerating and doing things that are not aligned with your values—which not only drains your energy but also doesn't move you toward the finish line of your goals. Here are a few values to get you started in thinking about this topic.

Achievement	Loyalty
Creativity	Power
Family	Reputation
Generosity	Respect
Honesty	Stability
Humor	Wealth
Love	Wisdom

Once you have a better understanding of what you are tolerating as it relates to your values, consider what else you are doing that is not serving you well. What else, if you really sat down and thought about it, could you live without? What else is taking up time that is not leading to excellence? Are you spending hours watching TV in the evening? Do you spend your commute time doing anything valuable like reading or listening to educational audio? Do you often say, "I don't have time for that"? Instead of saying, "I don't have time for that," say, "That is not my priority or not something I value," and move on to something that is your priority and in line with your values.

Once you have a handle on what is distracting you and what you are tolerating, you will start to say no to things and will get more done with less effort. You will leave work at the end of the day on time because you are done with your tasks. And you accomplished more than you ever did before, in less time! You will be able to find more work/life balance, and everything will be more fun and more rewarding.

If you need more help in understanding your distractions, go back to the idea of journaling, which I talked about in chapter 5. Actually write down your distractions. Track your time for a week. How much was spent on e-mail, putting out fires, and doing work that is not a priority or not in line with your values? How much time do you spend talking about the football game, what you watched on TV last night, or other non-money-generating, nonproductive activities? I'm not saying you can't be social at work, but when you start to see how much time you are spending on these activities, you begin to understand why you may feel like there are never enough hours in the day, or why you are always busy being busy without a lot of results to show for it.

Time to check in with yourself.

As it relates to this foundation:

1. What will happen if I do this?
2. What will happen if I don't do this?
3. What won't happen if I do this?
4. What won't happen if I don't do this?

CHAPTER 8

LEADERSHIP

What is *leadership* really? What kind of leader are you? How do others see you? What is your energy as a leader? How do you communicate? Are you blazing new trails or keeping the status quo alive and well?

"Leadership," what the *L* in the R.E.S.U.L.T.S. system stands for, can mean different things to different people. I cannot cover leadership in one chapter, nor do I want to try. This entire book is really about leadership and excellence, so I use this chapter to discuss a couple of ways that you, as a leader, can start to create a natural competitive advantage over others in your industry. This is about setting high standards and expectations, bringing in top talent, retaining them, and creating a strong culture.

⎯⎯ᴄ⎯⎯

Setting high standards and expectations will give everyone on your team a level playing field. These are the nonnegotiable rules that everyone must play by in order to have effective communication, synergy, productivity, and excellence.

Once you get started thinking about the standards you want your team and company to live by you will add many topics to your list. They may include integrity, honesty, fun, authenticity, focus, innovation, and so forth. These will be based on the culture you want to create and possibly a culture that does not yet exist or one that needs a radical transformation. Have you ever heard the ancient proverb "The fish rots from the head"? It means when an organization fails, the leadership is the root cause.

I will talk about culture shortly, but let me stop here to talk about my biggest pet peeve—and one that I bet is costing you a lot of money in lost productivity. It is the dirtiest word of all: multitasking. Yuk. I hate that word because it does not exist. You cannot multitask. It is not an asset, so please remove it from any job description you have because you do not want people who think they can multitask—they cannot.

What you think multitasking is and what actually happens are two very different things. You think it is someone who can efficiently do multiple things at once, but no one can, at least not two cognitive things at the same time. Sure, you can walk and chew gum at the same time, or talk and drive at the same time, but you cannot read e-mail and be on a conference call at the same time, or be in a meeting and responding to a text or an e-mail at the same time.

You see, in these last examples you are switching back and forth between the activities, you are not multitasking. You are doing multiple activities, but not at the same time. You are listening to the conference call and then you are reading an e-mail. You are participating in the meeting and then you are sending a text. You are not doing them si-multaneously, and if you think you are, you are losing a lot of money on productivity.

I remember vividly (because I was ready to kill this guy if only I hadn't been on the other end of a phone) a client who, during a conference call, would say, "I'm sorry, can you repeat that? I was multitasking," every time I asked him a question. *No, you asshole, I will not repeat it. Stop doing other things while you are on this call with me—and oh, by the way, you are not multitasking; you are being rude, causing this call to take longer, and you're hav-ing to pay me more to be here.* OK, fine, I didn't say that, but I sure wanted to. Instead, because I am a professional and was there as an information-security consultant, not a coach, I politely repeated myself and bit my tongue. If this person treats all conference calls or all business this way, think how much longer it takes him to get anything done.

At another client's office, everyone would sit down in the conference room (if they bothered to show up rather than call in from down the hall—probably so they could "multitask") with their cell phones on the table in front of them. I'm not sure why, since none of these folks were on call or had anything so important that it could not wait till the meet-ing was over. But company culture allowed this, and I don't know how many times someone would be on their phone, responding to a text or an e-mail, and look up and say, "Sorry, what?"

The practice resulted in wasted time and disrespect and, honestly, should not have been tolerated. What I've started to realize is that we have made technology so easy to access and so much a part of our lives, at work and at home, this kind of behavior is being allowed even though it is not a standard of excellence. We are in a world where people need people, not more technology. Let me say this loud and clear—PUT

THE TECHNOLOGY DOWN AND STEP AWAY. Start to pay attention and listen to those around you, communicate for real, ask questions, look for solutions, and change mind-sets. None of these actions require technology. Set a new standard that multitasking is not real, and that cell phones are not allowed in the conference room or boardroom (or dining room). Set the new expectation and follow through. Lead by example and keep your own cell phone in your office when you are in a meeting.

What about the concept of keyboard confidence? Saying things behind the safety of your computer that you would never say to someone in person or even on the phone. E-mail is being used, not as a productivity tool, but as a way to hide and treat people in a way that should never be tolerated. We don't know what is going on in most people's lives behind the scenes at home. It is time to start treating people like people and realizing that most business problems are really just people problems that can be easily corrected when standards are set high, expectations are communicated, and leaders lead by example. It's about leading with integrity, honesty, and compassion.

―⤶

Another topic to be addressed in a discussion on leadership is how hiring and retaining top talent translates to more engaged and more productive employees along with better profits and a natural competitive advantage. Who doesn't want to be the industry leader, make better profits, and do it with less effort and less stress?

Most hiring begins with a job description written in an HR-approved way or by someone who isn't actually the one who is doing the job. The job description does not describe the actual tasks or the amount of time each task will be performed during a day or week. Remember, this goes back to unique brilliance. Let's use a sales job as an example. Not all sales jobs are the same, and not all salespeople are wired the same way or created equal.

Someone who is wired to collaborate, see the vision of others, nurture and support others, and ask a lot of questions is very different from someone who likes routines and systems. Both these types of people can be great salespeople, but not in the same sales role. If you are hiring for an outside salesperson to nurture some client relationships that were weakened by the previous salesperson, you need the first type of person I described, not the second. If you are not describing your needs in the right details or understanding how your job candidates are wired (their unique brilliance), however, you may end up with the wrong person. When I say wrong, I don't mean they are bad employees or bad salespeople; I just mean they are not the energy you need for that specific job.

The job description is important, but the energy needed for the job is even more important. To bring in the best talent for each job every time, you need to match the core and wiring of the person you hire with the energy that's needed to do the job.

I know you are thinking this sounds like it will take a lot more time and cost more money, and you don't know whether it will even work. Those thoughts make sense; anything new can lead to worry or apprehension. My goal is not to make this hard for you, but rather to make it easy. That is why I am going to introduce you to my partners at Taylor Protocols Inc. who have created a systematic approach for putting the right people in the right seat. You may be rolling your eyes, thinking this is a shameless plug or sales pitch. Let me say this: my job is to provide you with value, ideas, solutions, and information. I do this from a place of love and integrity every time. I am very particular about who I do business with, and this stuff is just really cool. And since I do have the utmost respect for you, let's leave it at that for now. You can learn more about them at www.c-suiteresults.com or by visiting www.taylorprotocols.com. Tell them Sharon Smith sent you and they will take great care of you; that I promise.

⎯ᕋ

Leadership is also about hard conversations with good people when they are not doing a great job. But now that you know about unique brilliance, you can go into such conversations in a very different way. You can find out what it is that your employees like about their job and what it is they don't like. You can find out what they would do every day all day if they could. What are their passions and their strengths? You can help them uncover their unique brilliance using the tools I recommend in chapter 4 or any tool that works for you. Then you can see if the challenge with their performance is nothing more than being in the wrong job for the way they are wired. As I've mentioned, in my previous life I was really a great information-security consultant, but I didn't love the work I was doing. I loved part of it—the conversations, the communication, the getting to know each client's business, challenges, and desires. What I did not like at all was the reporting, the systematic approach to each assessment, and the detail-oriented requirements I had to fulfill.

What I would have really excelled at if I had known earlier was being a sales engineer. I could have used my strengths, gifts, and energies to still serve the same industries, but in a way that was more aligned with who I am.

The same holds true for your executive team. Do you have someone on your team, someone else in the C-Suite or a vice president or a director who is not performing up to standards? Someone whose department is not having the same results as other departments? I would bet that 80 percent of the time it has to do with people being in roles that do not support their unique brilliance or their unique energy recipe.

This is not an area to gloss over. Whether you use a tool like the ones I use or you do this another way, I beg you to start looking at the "who" in each person and the energy that the job he or she fills requires. It will make all your employees work harder because they will be doing work they love, work they are meant to do. It will result in better profits and better customer service, and your employees will be your number-one fans. They will talk about your company everywhere they go, and you will gain a natural competitive advantage without having to spend more money on marketing campaigns, PR experts, or a larger sales force. Your entire organization will be your sales force, even if they are not being paid for that role.

—6

The last topic for this chapter, but one I could probably write an entire book on, is company culture. You may not realize it, but you, as the senior executive, create the culture that exists in your company today. You may have been very specific in what you created, or it may have happened on its own over time without much thought.

It's time to give it thought and make changes where needed. What do you know about your current culture? If you were to define it, what would you say? Is there a culture of open communication, collaboration, integrity, fun, empowerment, hard work, and growth? Or is there a dog-eat-dog culture, with every man for himself? Is turnover high? What about employee engagement and satisfaction? Are employees encouraged to bring in new ideas or ridiculed for new thoughts? If you were to take a walk through the halls and cubes of your organization—yes, I mean leave your office and talk to people or listen like a fly on the wall—what would you hear?

Are your employees speaking highly of you and the rest of your team? Are they counting down the days till Friday? Do they feel empowered to go to their boss who has "an open-door policy," or is that all lip service? Are you walking the talk yourself? Make a list of everything you think your company culture is and then get serious about finding out how true it is. I don't mean just through surveys that no one takes seriously. I mean through real conversations, town hall meetings, or other means to get to the truth in a way that everyone feels safe and allowed to contribute. If you don't think anyone will speak the truth out of fear, then that is a cultural issue in and of itself.

Your culture is not just a part of what brings the best talent to work for you; it is also a huge part of leading and retaining top talent, customer satisfaction, and overall leadership within your industry. It's time to take a good, hard look at the culture you have created and determine whether it is a culture of excellence or a culture where everyone is just hanging in there, holding on for Friday.

Time to check in with yourself.

As it relates to this foundation:

1. What will happen if I do this?
2. What will happen if I don't do this?
3. What won't happen if I do this?
4. What won't happen if I don't do this?

CHAPTER 9

TAKE ACTION

Sometimes what stops a good leader from becoming a great leader is the inability to *take action* (the *T* in R.E.S.U.L.T.S. stands for "take"). All leaders, including most of you, have great ideas. But do you take action on those ideas? Do they seem big and scary or do you think, "How can I ever accomplish that?" When you feel overwhelmed, I know that it is easier to take no action than it is to start and maybe fail. I am no different in this department. I've had many great ideas that have gone nowhere out of fear, but I also know that when I do take action, breaking the idea down into manageable chunks, even the smallest action gets the ball rolling.

You have to start somewhere, and you can start small. Once the momentum builds, you are unstoppable. Once you do the first scary thing and it does not kill you (and it won't), it is easier to take the next step, and then the next. For example, I am in Ecuador as I write this, and I came on this trip as a working vacation because my life allowed it. It's scary to be in a place where you don't speak the language, however. Every day I do something new that at first is scary, but then I get to be proud of it and do it again and again until it becomes second nature.

You want to know how that relates to you and your business. You want to know how you can take action to move forward, so let's look at a business scenario. You can pick your own goal and work through it with this outline. Now, before I continue, please note this is not new information. I did not go to the ends of the earth to create something that has never been seen before. Actually, nothing in this book is new, but most great ideas are not. Napoleon Hill started writing about these topics a long time ago. Great leaders and business gurus have continued the teachings, and I am passing along what I have learned, implemented, and believe to you.

Most of these ideas are old ideas, presented to you in what I hope is a fresh way that inspires you to start making changes that will get you the results you want and deserve. If you have heard this three or more times from different people and never implemented it, the rule of three means it's time to get moving. When the same idea, opportunity, or theme shows up in your life for a third time, the Universe (yes, I said Universe) is telling you to start paying attention.

The way you are going to take action is by setting SMART goals, strategies, and tactics to move you forward in creating your excellence, the vision you put together in chapter 5, your dream life, the life you deserve. SMART stands for specific, measurable, actionable, realistic, and time centric (it has a specific end date or time frame).

Also, I should actually say that it isn't the goal itself that is SMART, it is each step in reaching the goal that has to be SMART. This is where most people mess up when it comes to goals or give up because the goal feels daunting. For example, say you want to make $100,000, or you want to have twenty-five clients, or you want a new car (or a new house, a new job, a new anything). Then you try to make a plan to reach that goal.

Unless the plan is supported by a strategy and then broken down into many steps (tactics), you have a slim chance in reaching that goal no matter how SMART the goal is. What you need to do is determine the strategy and tactics, and each tactic must be SMART.

I want to make this simple because in all reality that is how my mind works. When things get too theoretical for me, I'm lost or bored and distracted; that's just how I am wired, so that is how I will explain this concept. Let's use the goal of getting a new job. A lot of questions have to be asked and a lot of brainstorming has to be done before you can even start creating SMART tactics.

- Why do you want a new job (more money, greater responsibility, better location, better boss, better benefits, and so on)? I ask this because without knowing why, it will be easy to get distracted and easy to give up when it gets tough or when you don't get results fast. Also, without knowing why, you won't have a clear strategy.

- Let's say you want a job that is closer to home with better or more flexible hours. This is important because your strategy now includes where you are looking. You are not looking for a job anywhere; you are looking for a job in a very specific location with specific hours.

- Now you know that if you see a job that is outside your range but offers much more money than you currently make, it does not matter because it is not what you are looking for. It does not support your "why," and you will not let it distract you from your goal. Remember, when you understand what is distracting you, you can remove it.

- Strategy can include working with a headhunter, using a specific online search engine, going to job fairs, using the newspaper, using LinkedIn, and so on. You may include more than one strategy, but you should focus on only two or three strategies; otherwise, you are going to get distracted.

- Let's say in this case your strategies are using LinkedIn, going to local networking events in your industry, and working with a local headhunter specializing in your industry. Now you can look at the tactics for each strategy, and this is where you get SMART.

- Next, brainstorm all the steps you will need to take. The steps do not have to be in order yet; you just need to include everything that needs to be done. For example, find a headhunter to work with, find networking events, make new connections on LinkedIn, update your profile and resume, add a new profile picture and headline, write objectives specific to what you want to do, practice interviewing, get a new suit, print résumés, have a way of writing thank-you cards, pick a radius you want to work in, and so on.

- Now you need to start ordering these tasks, and you may even find new ones to add once you start to use the SMART strategy for each task. For example, in order to update your profile picture, you may need new pictures taken, which means adding a task to get headshots, and that may lead to another new step of finding a photographer.

- Now that you have your tasks—and yes, the list will grow—you want to ensure that each is specific. That is the *S* in SMART. You cannot just say you are going to apply to a lot of jobs or talk to a lot of people in your network this week. You need to get specific. You need to say you are going to talk to ten people in your LinkedIn network or to three recruiting organizations, or you are going to five networking events this week.

- The task also has to be measurable so you know when it is complete. Many things are not measurable, but five people, three companies, and ten applications are. You must be able to look at what you did and know when you are done. That is measurable.

- Is the task achievable? Do you have the resources you need to achieve the task? If the task is to go to five networking events this week but you don't have any events to go to, even though it is specific and measurable, it is not achievable. You may need to add the task of finding five networking events. Then the next task of attending them is achievable, assuming they are on days and at times when you can go. The task is not achievable if you do not have all the resources available to make it happen yet. Getting those resources may become additional steps or tactics.

- So, now you have a specific, measurable, and achievable task. Is it realistic? Will you actually do it? There is a big difference between knowing what to do—and even having the resources to do it—and doing it. If you have never worked out before, is it realistic on January 1 to say you're going to go to the gym every day for an hour? No, it's not realistic, because after two or three days of being sore and tired, you are going to stop. Is it realistic to say you are going to go on Monday, Wednesday, and Friday for the first two weeks? Yes, that is more realistic. On a scale of one to ten, with one being "No way will I ever do that" (for me, jumping out of a plane) and ten being "Hell yeah, I'll do that" (for me, going to Italy for a month), where are you on the scale of realism for each task? If you are not at a nine or ten, you need to revisit the task. What will it take to get you to the place of action for that task?

- Now, for the time frame of each task. Without a time frame of when you will do everything, how will you measure it or ever get it all done? Let's take the specific task of talking to ten people in your LinkedIn network. In what time frame is this? Over the next month, week, day? You need to choose a time frame that fits all the other pieces. Is it achievable (ten people in a day versus ten people in a week)? Is it realistic (do you have time to do this, and will you)?

- Now you have to do this for every task, some of which may be done at the same time and some of which may need to be done before others. Start ordering the tasks and making each one SMART.

- Now that you have your project plan, find those you need to help you, get those who have unique brilliance in areas you don't, and make sure the tasks and people align with your priorities, vision, and values.

Now it's your turn. What is one thing you have been putting off? What is something that has gone undone at work or at home? What is something, no matter how small, you can apply taking action to *right now*? Go ahead; have fun with it. Use your unique brilliance, remove those energy blocks, remove distractions, ask for help, get vulnerable, create a vision, stay present, and *take action*!

Time to check in with yourself.

As it relates to this foundation:

1. What will happen if I do this?
2. What will happen if I don't do this?
3. What won't happen if I do this?
4. What won't happen if I don't do this?

CHAPTER 10

SIMPLIFY

I think I saved the best and shortest chapter for last. When you *simplify* (which the final *S* in R.E.S.U.L.T.S. stands for) your work and your life, all of a sudden you have work/life balance, less stress, and less pain. Plus, because you will be working smarter, so will your team and your organization. When you put all of this together and consistently implement these ideas and strategies, you will make more money and see better overall results.

This means you will focus only on your priorities—the tasks that align with your values and that you are uniquely brilliant to deal with—and you delegate *everything* else. Yes, I mean everything else. You say no to anything and everything that does not align with what you are working on—with your big rocks, your vision, your "why," your excellence, your priorities, your values, and your brilliance.

A trait of a great leader is the ability to empower others. One decision you can make now to avoid future pain is to stop thinking that you can do everything yourself or that no one can do it better than you can. Also, when you believe that not having the answers is a sign of weakness, you ignore your team and their brilliance. When you think you are the only one who knows best, you are setting yourself up to work harder with fewer results, less profit, and more pain. Many executives and nonexecutives choose to think this way on a daily basis, all of which you can avoid.

Now, I'm not a fan of the word "mistake," so that is why I said "choose to think this way" rather than "make the mistake of thinking this way." I think we all do things the best way we can with the tools and knowledge we have at the time. It is only a mistake if we decide we don't need to improve, if we decide we don't need to be more self-aware, and if we don't learn from the actions we took.

Whether an action resulted in something we wanted or something we did not want, we can learn from it. When we do something that works once but never do it again, we show that we did not learn, and that great outcome was pretty much a wasted event. When we do learn from what worked before, we can repeat those actions and get more and more great results.

The same is true when we do not get the result we wanted. We can be mad about it, we can blame someone else or blame our circumstances, but at the end of the day, we must take full responsibility for all outcomes, including the ones that worked and the ones that did not work.

Instead of seeing mistakes, I encourage you to do the following exercise after a project or decision has been completed. It's a tool you can use to review anything, whether it was a business decision or a life decision. Grab a piece of paper, make four columns, and label them as follows:

- The first column: "What Worked"
- The second column: "What Didn't Work"

- The third column: "What Could We Do Differently Next Time?"
- The fourth column: "New Standards We Will Implement Going Forward"

The point of this exercise is to learn what went well and what did not go so well and then adjust plans, standards, and expectations accordingly in the future. It is a simple way to move from a mind-set of making mistakes to one of learning, changing, and growing. I've put this together for you in the companion download to the book at www.c-suiteresults.com.

Other actions that do not often result in great outcomes include not fully understanding a situation before coming up with answers, opinions, and ideas; talking more than you listen (we all know that we have two ears and one mouth, so why do most people talk more than they listen?); focusing only on dollars and the bottom line instead of focusing on people; and trying to save money by hiring less expensive resources instead of learning how to hire and retain top talent.

These are but a few "mistakes" or decisions that are made on a daily basis in boardrooms across the country. These decisions matter because they do not lead to excellence in the boardroom, and they definitely won't lead you to greatness or excellence beyond the boardroom.

Everything that is simple to do is simple *not* to do. It takes a great leader to start implementing these steps. Even taking one step at a time will make a difference, and over time you will start to see exponential results. Often the fastest way to simplify things is to work with an expert, someone who has already taken the time to put the system together—someone whose unique brilliance is creating excellence, shifting mind-sets, and helping you create an organization and a life of unparalleled excellence.

Just like I should not do my accounting books, my filing, or my administrative work because these things are far outside my unique brilliance, I encourage you to work with someone who gets energy out of working with you on these topics.

Can I help you reveal your unique brilliance? (If not me, find someone who is a good fit for you, your company, and your challenges.) Feel free to stop by and visit me at www.c-suiteresults.com, where you can download your companion documents, learn more about who I am and the tools I use, contact me, and take the free CVI assessment I've made available on the resource page.

Time to check in with yourself.

As it relates to this foundation:

1. What will happen if I do this?
2. What will happen if I don't do this?
3. What won't happen if I do this?
4. What won't happen if I don't do this?

About the Author

After fifteen years of working in different industries to include federal government, internal audit, and then as an information-security consultant and subject-matter expert, it became clear that I was not where I belonged. I had too many cases of the Sunday-night blues for too many years. I was not doing work that gave me joy or energy, and now that I have studied and understand this, that makes perfect sense. You see, we are all born with unique gifts and different combinations of energies that make up who we are. Once we understand this, we can align our work with our unique brilliance, and everything becomes easier, more fun, and more rewarding.

The journey from unfulfilled employee to engaged business owner took some time. When I found coaching, I finally started doing work that filled me up and gave me a sense of purpose, joy, and energy. Those fifteen disengaged and dissatisfying years could have been avoided if I had known how I was wired or what my unique brilliance was when I was picking my college major in accounting at seventeen, or when I was picking my graduate degree in computer forensics at twenty-three. But I didn't have the tools back then, and I chose wrong.

During my journey I found coaching and went to the Institute for Professional Excellence in Coaching, where I spent over three hundred hours sharpening my saw to become a certified professional coach. I also studied energy leadership and received the Energy Leadership Index Master Practitioner, or ELI-MP, certification.

I partnered with Taylor Protocols Inc. in order to bring the Core Values Index to corporate America and help individuals and leaders understand their unique brilliance and how they are wired. Because I now know how I am wired and that I could have used that information much earlier to have a more rewarding career, I am on a mission to help as many people as I can uncover their brilliance and understand how they are wired.

I am passionate about change, especially change in how corporate America functions. Too many people (employees and leaders) are dragging themselves into work every day, doing work that is not in alignment with who they are, and leaving at the end of the day drained and feeling pretty darn bad. That is no way to live, so I have created the C-Suite R.E.S.U.L.T.S. system. Just because employee engagement averages around 32 percent does not mean it has to stay so low. As a leader, you have a responsibility to start doing things differently! It is time to become the next-generation leader that we so desperately need. You can either keep doing what you have always done and keep getting the same results, or you can change. Yes, I know from personal experience that change can be painful, but I also know that it can be very rewarding. It's time to contact me so we can talk about the changes you want, need, and are ready for.

Sharon Smith

sharon@c-suiteresults.com

www.c-suiteresults.com

LinkedIn https://www.linkedin.com/in/smithsharonj

Made in the USA
Columbia, SC
01 May 2018